The Positive Positive Negative Positive Principle

The Positive Positive Negative Positive Principle:
Writing Social Scripts for Students with
Autism Spectrum Disorders

Published by
Condict-Cochran
Geneva, IL

ISBN 978-0-6151-7523-2

This book is dedicated to my loving and supportive family: My husband, Bud for keeping Cody busy when I had to write, my son, Cody for keeping Daddy busy when I had to write, my parents, Wayne & LaVada for all their love and support and my sister Kari for always being just a phone call away.

About the Author

Chelley Condict-Cochran, Ed. D. has spent eighteen years of her professional life in the field of Special Education. Over the past 10 years, she has had an educational emphasis on Pervasive Developmental Disorders. She held positions in Hawaii, Florida, and Illinois as a special education teacher, inclusion facilitator, and autism facilitator. She holds a Bachelor's Degree in Learning Disabilities and Educable Mental Handicap, a Master's of Science in Education for Varying Exceptionalities, and a Doctorate of Education in Child, Youth, and Family Studies for Special Services. Chelley is currently an Autism Facilitator for a school district in Northern Illinois. Dr. Cochran provides on-site training, identification, behavior management, and programming for teachers of students with autism and other Pervasive Developmental Disorders.

Preface

Over the past 10 years, providing social instruction and behavior management to students identified with an Autism Spectrum Disorder (ASD) or various other Pervasive Developmental Disorders has been my professional point of concentration. I believe in providing students with age and grade appropriate supports to assist them in surviving the social agenda of the schools. My role as an Autism Facilitator enables me to introduce teachers to various visual supports such as schedules, social stories, and social scripts. I encourage the teachers to create and utilize these supports for their students.

What I have found is that frequently the teachers would leave me voice mail messages or send email messages asking me to write the social script for them because they were not sure where to start. The teachers could identify what behavior they wanted to change, but did not know how to put it down on paper. In efforts to empower the teachers, I set out to teach the teachers how to write the social scripts or principles. What I discovered was I frequently asked the teachers if they could be more positive. Many of their earlier attempts were based on what behavior the student would not engage. No touching. No talking. No hitting. Each behavior, although a valid concern for the classroom teacher, did little to teach the student the appropriate behavior.

I wanted the students using these social principles to like what they were reading and use it as an effective behavior management tool. I find that children and adults are motivated more by being informed of what should be done and less of what not to do. I began to ask teachers, could the directive be stated in a positive manner? Would it be possible to only state the behavior you **do** want and not the behavior you **do not**? I kept asking for more positives, more positives, and more positives.

I wondered how I could make writing social scripts more concrete for the teachers. Then it occurred to me; a social strategy I had been taught several years ago as a young girl at a well known charm school! I remembered the proper way to decline an invitation or tell someone no was to be positive in thanking them for the invitation, decline the request, and then be positive again by wishing them an enjoyable time at the event without you. To me, this is one of the nicest ways to be told no.

Isn't that what we are often trying to tell our ASD students? No. No talking. No hitting. No arguing. Why wouldn't this formula work for them? So I wrote a few examples and practiced with several students until a formula was created. Positive, positive, negative, positive! It is easy to learn, easy to perfect, and easy to implement. I hope you can find it useful, too!

Yours Respectfully,

Chelley

Acknowledgements

I would like to acknowledge the educators who so willingly implemented my suggestions enabling us to develop a program successful for the children. I would also like to thank the parents and their children with autism for allowing me to share this learning experience with them. In addition, I would not have been as effective if I had not had the support from other professionals I consider my friends.

Table of Contents

Introduction

The Positive, Positive, Negative, Positive (++-+) Principle is a strategy designed to assist students succeed in life. It provides Autism Spectrum Disorder (ASD) students with an internal voice. It is a simple formula created to enable teachers, parents, care givers, a means to take an abstract concept and produce a concrete directive. When looking at the diagnostic criteria of the DSM-IV pervasive development disorders, three distinct characteristics make up a child with 299.00 Autistic disorder; qualitative impairment in social interaction, qualitative impairment in communication, and restricted repetitive and stereotyped patterns of behavior, interests, and activities. The ++-+ Principle addresses each of these three areas for a child with autism.

One identifying characteristic of children with autism is impairment in social interactions. Social interactions for children on the spectrum can be extremely difficult. The entire social agenda of society is an unwritten game in which we all must participate. Use of the ++-+ Principle can break down a completely illogical behavior and make it concrete and sequential for the child with autism. A verbal prompt as abstract as 'calm down' is to an ASD student, now becomes observable, measurable, repeatable and teachable.

A second characteristic is impairment in expressive and or receptive communication. Many students have difficulty retrieving the language they are attempting to communicate. Word retrieval, sentence fluency, and intended meaning all get lost in the mind of a child with autism. The ++-+ Principle enables the child to practice, memorize, utilize, and generalize language and behaviors needed to effectively communicate with others. In addition, it assures that all adults working with this child use the same language and strategy to assist in creating a successful learning environment.

The third is a restricted or repetitive behavioral interest. The ++-+ Principle can also assist in behavior shaping identified undesirable behaviors that students may exhibit. Students can be taught replacement behaviors, anxiety decreasing behaviors, or socially acceptable behaviors in a much prescribed manner. Behavior shaping is necessary to aid students in meeting the social expectations of the educational system as well. Students with ASD are taught strategies on how to behave in certain social or academic situations.

The ++-+ Principle also can improve the social interactions of the children with ASD and the non-disabled peers. As the social skills of the ASD student improve, non-disabled peers are better able to engage in joint conversations or activities. In many of my classes, the principles are read and/or shared with peers. This open form of communication builds tolerance and sets the expectations of all behaviors in the class.

Chapter One: The + + - + Principle Strengths

The ++-+ Principle is very easy to learn, practice, and implement. Yet, it is extremely powerful and effective. One positive factor is that this principle provides ASD students with an *internal voice*. This is the little voice inside all of us which helps us survive. Unfortunately, it is often very quiet or silent in children with ASD. This little voice tells us we can tolerate a situation for a length of time. It may tell us not to behave a certain way or to behave in another way. The psychologists among us call this the ego process. Often our internal voice can be the pusher, the pleaser, the critic or the perfectionist. The ++-+ Principle helps reign in the negative or absent ego voice and encourages the student to be successful. However it is not just words because we incorporate taught behavior strategies for the ASD students.

Another added benefit of the ++-+ Principle is it improves expressive and receptive communication. As with any visual support, we have a better understanding of the message the ASD child is attempting to communicate. We are also capable of now providing them with specific taught strategies to compensate for the behavior or feeling. When we pair the written and spoken word, we increase the ASD child's understanding of what behavior they should be exhibiting. It is further supported in that the ++-+ Principle uses clear and consistent language which can be taught in many settings. Use of a principle can assist students in coping with their own anxiety.

When working with students with ASD, the use of strategies to help them develop, generalize, and maintain pragmatic language and communication skills is essential. The strategies utilized in given situations will vary depending on the emotional and behavioral needs of the students. It is also necessary to consider the intellectual ability of the student to match skill levels. The strategies included in Chapter Nine of this book help students deal with the difficulties of paraverbal, nonverbal, and ambiguous language. The ++-+ Principle encourages the use of both receptive and expressive language.

Breakdown of communication occurs for a variety of reasons, including the message is not received at all, the message is received but not fully comprehended, or the message is received and comprehended but not responded to appropriately. Information breakdowns can also be impacted by environmental distractions or the use of overly complex communication signals or language. Attention issues and overly complex social context further destroy communication. These social breakdowns multiply if the ASD student is unable to make necessary adjustments or ask for clarification.

The ++-+ Principle assists both sides of the communication breakdown in better understanding one another. The use of this visual and verbal support clarifies the behavior or communicative message intended for the ASD student. This principle also provides the non-disabled person with the correct language and strategy to help deescalate a particular behavior.

The ++-+ Principle also can be used to illicit a positive behavior or to stop an inappropriate behavior. It is all in the wording of the Principle. For most negative behaviors, we attempt to decrease the intensity and provide a replacement behavior. However, sometimes the principle will be used to teach an appropriate behavior for a specific situation. Perhaps a new procedure is being introduced into the class. A ++-+ Principle can easily let the student know of the change and the corresponding positive behavior expected.

Chapter Two: Creating a Principle: Step 1

Ok so everything sounds great so far, right. Now you want to start writing. But wait; there are a few procedural issues we have to cover. First, you must have a true understanding of the behavior you are observing. You must identify the core issue of the behavior. Often too many behaviors are addressed in one social skill lesson. In efforts to create a more effective teaching process, it is necessary to isolate one primary behavior to address at a time. It is also important to be specific when behavior shaping. Now is not the time to plan on changing three or four behaviors. Select one which would make the most impact first and build from there.

One method I suggest is to interview the other professionals involved with the student. This will assist you in determining if the behavior is global or isolated to your setting.

Here are a few example questions to ask the team. You will probably have additional questions specific to your ASD student.

- What does the student gain from this behavior?

- What is the most impacting behavior you see at this time?

- Where does it happen?

- How does the student/audience react?

- Is there a replacement behavior that would serve the same purpose?

- Is there a sensory component?

- How long does the behavior occur?

- What is the intensity?

- Can you recognize the behavior at the onset?

- What is the student's motivation for exhibiting this behavior?

If the behavior is complex, isolate one component to start behavior shaping. If the behavior is multi-dynamic, create a hierarchy of the steps involved in the behavior. In identifying the steps, prioritize areas to be addressed. From the priorities, determine which behavior change would be most impacting and create a social principal for that particular behavior.

Use this behavior as the foundation to build upon in creating an entire behavioral change. Once the initial principle is mastered, reevaluate the behavior and again select a priority to address in the next principle. Only address additional behaviors once the foundation has been established and the level of acceptable mastery has been achieved.

I am very data driven. Education often responds to thoughts or ideas without concrete data to support the recent movement or latest trend. For students with ASD, the data becomes documentation for us to create programs and manage behaviors. When you are faced with changing a behavior, gather your data. Expect this documentation from your team as well. The data can be as simple as attendance records or behavior write-ups, but it should also include time-sweeps or event recording.

From this data, generate a draft of what you think is the primary behavioral issue. If there is no data or the data is insufficient, observations must be conducted prior to writing a principle. During your observations, collect the data and encourage other teachers working with the ASD student to collect the same data. This data will drive the foundation of the principle. It is very difficult to determine if your strategy is effective if there is no baseline data. Do not skip this step.

Next, begin to brainstorm replacement behaviors that would serve the same function for the student without the inappropriate behavior. Think about how this can be stated as an affirmation. What would the preferred behavior look like? What behavior is the rest of the class expected to exhibit? What behavior is impossible to do simultaneously to the inappropriate behavior? What you have created here is the hypothesis for the target behavior. This is the basis of diminishing the undesired behavior and shaping the desired behavior.

Sample hypothesis statements:

Think of your ABCs-antecedent, behavior, and consequences when writing the hypothesis. The **Antecedent** causes the student to **Behave** a certain way to serve as a particular **Consequence** or function.

- When having to speak out in class, student will destroy materials in order to be removed from the classroom. This is most likely to occur because the student is experiencing anxiety.

- When having to wait to have a turn, student will blurt answers aloud in order to speak before everyone else. This is most likely to occur because the student does not have coping skills for waiting.

- When presented with a test taking situation, student begins to cry in order to be removed from the classroom and take the test in another setting. This is most likely to occur because the student is nervous about failing the test.

To the best of our knowledge, this is the root of the behavioral concern for the student. We may have to collect additional data to confirm or deny this hypothesis.

Chapter Three: Creating the Principle: Step 2

With your hypothesis in hand, the next crucial component is to interview the student themselves. I have had great success with this strategy. Many of the students I have worked with like to feel in control. Allowing them to an opportunity express their point of view often makes them more willing to participate in the implementation of the principle because they helped write it!

Consider having several people interview the student to get a true picture of the behavior and perhaps why it is occurring. From the varying answers, hidden or underlying messages can be generated from the student's responses. Let's be honest, sometimes the students have more behavior problems in one class than they do in another. I can develop a plan to better help the student from knowing where there are higher levels of frustration; even if that means in one particular class.

Some sample questions I have used are:

1. What do you or don't you like about _____(subject/teacher).

2. How do you act in this class?

3. How do the other students act?

4. What would be the right behavior?

5. Do you know the rules of _____? (class/subject)

6. What do you feel is the problem?

7. How would you describe the behavior?

8. When, where, why, with whom, etc. does this behavior occur?

9. What choices do you have to behave?

10. When you are angry/ nervous, what makes you feel better?

11. What are the words that you would use to calm yourself?

12. What behaviors do you do to calm themselves?

You are the investigator now. At this time, document the student's choice of words to use in describing the behavior or the problem. Also, interpret emotions the student is conveying. If this topic makes them very nervous or agitated, use this information to create a non-threatening principle. If the behavior being addressed is of silliness, and the student begins to escalate just being interviewed about the topic, be prepared to create a directive principle. Ultimately, the information you gather from the student will assist you in creating the most effective principle. The more accurate your information is now, the more effective your principle will be later.

Sometimes the student may express that they have no concerns for this behavior. If this is the case, you may have to pre-teach some social skills. The student may be oblivious to the disruption their behavior is causing the class. Before a change can be made, they must be made aware of their behavior. When this happens, I often go back to the classroom teacher and see if we can better identify an antecedent to put some additional supports into place.

If all else fails, I ultimately present the principle as a class rule. Many of my students have responded successfully to the principles when they think of it as an expectation and not an option. I only use this as a last resort if all of my other strategies have failed. I am all about focusing on the positive!

If the student is nonverbal, you may consider interviewing parents, caregivers, or siblings, in efforts to get the students perspective. The therapists the student works with can also provide additional insight to the behavior the student is exhibiting. I use the visual choice boards in helping determine items preferred and less preferred. Although it is more time consuming when the student is non-verbal, a quality principle still can be developed and implemented. I have included a few examples in Chapter Nine.

Chapter Four: Creating a Principle: Step 3

The ++-+ Principle is a tool for the student to utilize therefore; the language of the principle should be commensurate with the individual's cognitive ability. This is easily generated once the student's input is provided. Our students with the 'Little Professor' language will appreciate a Principle written with terms they would use in speaking. Students requiring illustrations or real life pictures will respond to that visual in turn.

Utilize visuals paired with the written language when appropriate. The students with limited language can be instructed with the use of visual supports in the form of digital pictures or clip-art drawings. There is no cut off age for incorporating pictures into the Principle. In addition, there is no requirement for illustrations in younger children. However, be sure to include the written language in all principles so that each person implementing the principle will respond with the same language. This allows for consistency and better comprehension for the ASD student.

Pair the support with the student's ability and interest level. This is sometimes difficult due to the actual behavior being addressed. If the behavior itself is immature, we sometimes slip into using less mature language. In order for this to be most effective, the language has to match the students' ability. It is especially important because this principle should be used in several settings with several different people. We should always be respectful of our students and their ability.

I also have paired high interest topics with principles if I needed to motivate the student to attend to the principle. However, I use this selectively due to the ability of some of our students to hyper-attend. It is at your discretion if a motivator is needed. If the motivator takes away from the desired outcome of the principle, I would recommend not using one.

The next important component is to utilize language in the active tense. The principle is to be a form of a cheerleader encouraging the student to do the behavior and that they are capable of doing it! Avoid the use of negatives. It is far too easy to just list several behaviors of which we do not want the student to engage. We are creating an internal voice for these students. This must be positive, encouraging, and above all attainable! Remember, we want them to use this tool readily. It is in our and their best interest to make it as appealing as possible.

Another means of making the principle appealing is the actual media on which the principle is created. Consider various materials if it is appropriate for your student. I have used such items as laminated card stock, poster board, felt board, sticky notes, notebook paper, index cards, photo paper, wallets, and photo albums. You could use magnets, Velcro, song and dance, and so much more! Be creative in designing an appealing principle.

Chapter Five: Creating the Principle: Step 4

The formula:

Positive, Positive, Negative, Positive (++-+)

+ Topic

+ Refine the topic.

- State the behavior desired or expected.

+ Provide positive feedback.

At the beginning of this book I shared with you how I came about this formula. It is simply put, the polite way to tell someone no. It is my goal to be able to have the students to be in control of their own behavior and not rely on another person telling them how to behave. If in conducting a classroom observation, I tally 14 times in 10 minutes that a teacher said 'no...' to as ASD student, it would be obvious to me that a different strategy would be needed to change the undesired behavior. Although the formula is simplistic, it is important that the purpose of each component is explained in detail.

Positive (+): State one behavior or idea. This is the topic based on the data you collected about the student and the challenging behavior. This is also my attention getter. I want the student to want to read this principle. I set the stage and get the student to focus on the topic at hand.

Positive (+): State a second positive directly related to the identified behavior. This may include a setting, time, people, or other more specific details about the behavior requiring change. Here I often state what other students or people do in the same situation. This is in an attempt to create awareness that the behavior is expected of most people, including themselves!

Negative (-): State the behavior challenge as an affirmation. This is the behavior needing to be changed. The reason it is the negative, is because this is the part of the principle that will cause the student the most stress or difficulty. However, it is still stated in the active tense as the behavior desired or expected.   I include here what strategy I have determined that the student should apply. Reaffirm the student's ability to cope with the identified behavior based on a taught strategy. Include the possibility of relaxation, sensory integration, and coping skills which could all be taught to the ASD student.

Positive (+): Conclude the principle with words of encouragement about the student's ability to handle or cope with the behavior being addressed.

Chapter Six: Implementation

Once the initial principle has been written, you must begin to teach it to the student. First, read the paragraph with the student. Use inflection in your voice and in your manners to assist in assigning meaning to the words. Remember, subtlety is not a social strength of students with ASD. It is our job to provide direct instruction in teaching these mannerisms. Read the principle aloud. Use the visual to support what you are saying. Have the student follow along as you point to each word in the principle. Now, this should be something the student recognizes because their input was a part of creating this principle.

The next step is to read the principle together. Listen to the student's inflection. Does it mirror what the message is trying to convey? If not, practice this together until the student is able to successfully convey the paraverbals of the message.

Next, it is time for the student read the principle alone. You are watching for the student's ability to accurately read through the principle. Does the language match the student's ability? Is there a flow issue that needs to be addressed so that it is easier for the student to read? Are there added visual supports necessary for the student to better understand the expectations of the principle? As you analyze this information, you are determining if this principle is ready for continued implementation.

If you and the student are satisfied with the final product of the principle, it is time to share it with all others involved with the student. Most students do not attend school in a vacuum. They often have two, three, even four adults working with them on a regular basis. These additional adults should be taught the principle. You will have to model how it should be read to the students. It is also necessary to give examples as to when the principle should be used. Explain why the behavior is a problem and the proper response to the student's behavior. Also, explain how it is their role to enable the student to succeed in this setting. In efforts to generalize the behavior, this principle should be utilized across the student's entire day in many settings. This is especially important for nonverbal children as the principle will be read to them in each use.

Take the time to read principle prior to the challenging behavior or setting. If it is a time for transition, read the principle before the transition. If going to mainstream is a problem, read the principle before going to the mainstream class. If group activities cause behavior problems for the ASD student, read the principle before group and take a copy to group to refer to during the lesson. If coming in from recess is the issue, the recess teacher must have a copy to share with the student during recess. This principle is a working document. It should be visible and utilized frequently. On many occasions, it is even appropriate for students to read the principle to other students. Use your professional judgment to determine which topics are appropriate for students to share with one another.

Chapter Seven: Data Collection

Now that you have shared this principle with all the individuals involved with the targeted student, it is time to monitor its implementation. Collecting data throughout implementation is just as important as the data you collected prior to writing the principle. Utilize data collection to monitor the successfulness of the principle.

There are several types of data that can be collected. However, at this point we will focus on event recording and outcome data. Ultimately, we want to determine if the principle is working. In order to do this, we have to know who is implementing the principle, where it is being used, and the behavior of the student.

Event data, simply put, is recording when a targeted behavior occurs. Tally marks are most often utilized for this type of data collection. Set it up with your team as to how often this data should be collected and shared. At the onset of the principle, more frequent data should be collected. This serves two purposes…how often the student is presented with the principle and who is actually using the principle with the student. A thorough review of the event data will function as the overall baseline or outcome data.

Event Data Example:

Target Behavior: Talking out in class		
1.	2.	3.
4.	5.	6.
Intervals: 30 minutes per block		

Tally marks are recorded in each block to represent the number of talk-outs the student exhibited in a 30 minute session.

An unflattering side of education is a need to become the teacher police. We hate to admit it, but sometimes we have to help hold our teachers accountable. If your data indicates a certain individual is not implementing the principle, you will have to speak to that person individually. Take the time to explain how their participation in implementing this principle could make the difference in improving the behavior of the ASD student. Review the principle with them and see if they need suggestions on how to implement it in their setting. Maybe a modified product would be better for that setting. It is okay to individualize as long as the message is the same and it is for the benefit of the student.

Review the data and adjust the principle accordingly. Ideally, you will see a decrease in an unwanted behavior or an increase in a desired behavior. Monitor your data for this trend.

Keep in mind that there is an implementation dip when new strategies are introduced. Collect data for a few weeks and evaluate the pattern created. If the results are favorable, continue to document and explore simplifying further to fade this principle.

If it is not working, revisit step 1 to 4. Maybe the target behavior is not the real problem and it is necessary to go back to the beginning to redefine the target behavior. Or maybe the selected replacement behavior is not effective? Consider a different replacement behavior for the principle. Again, this is a working document. It changes and responds to the needs of the student. Allow the data to assist in the implementation of the principle.

If after several weeks, your data indicates that this behavior is nearly mastered. Move to fading the principle. Begin with decreasing the size of the visual support of the principle. Perhaps you will go from a 5X8 index card to a 3X5. Maybe the sentences will be reduced from 6 to 4. Determine if it is possible to eliminate some of the icons if pictures were used. The focus is to keep a reminder for the student to exhibit the appropriate behavior without having to read the entire principle. It is our goal to make this a permanent behavioral change. Continue fading the support in all settings. Ultimately, a one word prompt or icon will be all that is needed to illicit the appropriate response from the student.

What I recommend is that mastered principles be stored in student's own book of principles. This is a great tool for the students to see the level of behavioral growth they have achieved. The students enjoy seeing what they used to have problems about and how much they have grown. It gives them a great sense of accomplishment and it empowers them to continue making behavioral growth.

As teachers, we have concrete data on behaviors addressed and strategies found to be successful with our students. These books can travel with the students as they leave the elementary school to go to middle school and from middle school to go to high school. Therapists would benefit from this type of documentation for use in portfolio assessment as well.

Chapter Eight: Strategies for the Negative

In the ++-+ Principle, everything is focused on being positive. However, the challenge is to shape the negative behavior. The most important piece to remember about the negative is it must be a strategy taught to the student. Let's face it, if the negative behavior was an easy fix, you would not need to be writing a behavioral principle!

It is very important to work as a team addressing the challenging behaviors.   Utilize your resources available to you. Tap into the knowledge of the speech pathologist, social worker, occupational therapist, physical education teacher, physical therapist, classroom teacher, parent, principle, and more!

Strategies can take many shapes and forms. Some will be supported with props while others will simply be written language. Some varying examples are provided for you to begin to think outside of the box as to what might be beneficial for your student. Each strategy is appropriate for use in writing a principle.

Suggested Strategy Topics

- ✓ Activity alertness
- ✓ Ball chair
- ✓ Bean bag chair
- ✓ Body language
- ✓ Breathing
- ✓ Calming exercises
- ✓ Counting
- ✓ Draw
- ✓ Drink water
- ✓ Edible
- ✓ Exercise
- ✓ Eye contact
- ✓ Face speaker
- ✓ Listening therapy
- ✓ Low lights
- ✓ Jump on mini-tramp
- ✓ Music
- ✓ Peer support
- ✓ Point systems
- ✓ Raise hand
- ✓ Read
- ✓ Safe spot
- ✓ Schedules
- ✓ Self management
- ✓ Sensory integration specific to student's profile
- ✓ Squeeze whole body
- ✓ Social skills training
- ✓ Stretching
- ✓ Support person
- ✓ Swing
- ✓ Time out
- ✓ Turn card
- ✓ Visual supports
- ✓ Walking
- ✓ Weighted vest
- ✓ Wiggle seat

Chapter Nine: Examples

Here are a select few examples of principles taught to ASD students. For the first few principles, I have included the ++-+ code for you to have a better feel for the flow of the principle. The remaining principles address older students and you will see that a few have double positive (+) or double negative (-) to better communicate the expectation to the student.

I have placed these on individual pages for you to copy for students if necessary. However, I have found that it is more effective to write the principle with the student as described in chapter Three: Step 2 of creating the principle.

Although I have presented several written examples without visuals, I strongly encourage use of visuals within your examples. I encourage you to select visuals that are age and grade appropriate for your individual students. There are several commercial programs that will automatically fill in pictures or illustrations to match the words.

Talking Out

I enjoy discussions in my class. (+)

I often have great ideas to contribute. (+)

I will raise my hand to be called on to share my idea. (-)

I will be calm while I wait for my turn. (+)

Talking Out II

I enjoy discussions in my class. (+)

I often have great ideas to contribute. (+)

I like it when the teacher calls on me. (+)

I will raise my hand to be called on to share my idea. (-)

Sometimes I will have to wait for another turn to be called on. (-)

I will be calm while I wait for my turn. (+)

Taking Turns

I like to play Connect Four. (+)

Connect Four is fun when it is played with two people. (+)

After I put in my chip, my partner will put in his chip. (+)

I will wait for my partner to put in his chip. (-)

I will get another turn after my partner. (+)

This is how I play Connect Four! (+)

Taking Turns Talking in Class

Learning in school is fun! (+)

Answering questions and sharing information about the lesson are good ways to learn. (+)

My teacher calls on students who raise their hand. (+)

If I want to speak I raise my hand and wait to be called on. (+)

I can say to myself, "I know I can wait without talking." (-)

If I am not called on and I am disappointed, I can calm down by taking a deep breath, counting to 10 or doing the turtle. (-)

I will try again next time. It is fair when we all take turns! (+)

Staying Calm

I am in 5th grade. (+)

I go to school with many boys and girls. (+)

Sometimes, I may feel shy, confused, or frustrated. I need to calm down. (-)

I can squeeze my stress ball 5 times and say to myself, "I am calm." (-)

Then I can do my work and keep on learning. (+)

I can also ask my teacher for help if I need it! (+)

My teacher likes to help me when I am calm. (+)

Accepting NO for an Answer

I am growing up. (+)

At school students follow directions. (+)

At times I will be told no to something that I ask to do. (-)

I am told no because what I am asking may not be fair to others.
(-)

If I become upset, I can take a deep breath and squeeze my
stress ball to calm down. (-)

Everyone needs to learn to accept being told no. (+)

Accepting a no is part of growing up and getting along with
others. (+)

Accepting a no makes life fair for everyone. I like being fair. (+)

Asking for Help

Going to school helps me learn new things. (+)

I like to learn new things. (+)

Sometimes, I may not understand the directions or know what to do. (+)

I will ask for help. I will raise my hand. (-)

When I am called on, I can say, "Would you please help me with my work?" (-)

Teachers at school will help me understand my work. (+)

This is how I learn new things at school! (+)

Feeling Angry

I have lots of feelings. (+)

It is okay to feel angry. (+)

We all feel angry at times. (+)

When I feel angry, I will try to calm down. (-)

I can find a quiet place and talk about why I am mad. (-)

I am in control of my anger. (+)

I make good choices to calm down when I am angry. (+)

Feeling Frustrated

When I go to school, I want to do my best. (+)

Sometimes school work is very hard. (+)

I try and try to do my work. (+)

When I cannot do my work, I may feel frustrated. (-)

When I feel frustrated, it is helpful for me to relax. (-)

I can take a deep breath, count to 10, do the turtle, or do the rag doll. (-)

After I relax, I can try again. (+)

This makes me a good student. (+)

Making Mistakes

I go to school to learn new things. (+)

Sometimes learning involves making mistakes. (+)

If I am upset about making a mistake, I can take a deep breath to calm down. (-)

I can say to myself, "It is okay to make mistakes. Everyone makes mistakes." (-)

After I calm down, I stop thinking about the mistake and I move on with my work. (-)

Making a mistake teaches me what to do differently next time. (+)

It makes me a good student. (+)

My Schedule

Usually my schedule at school is the same every day. (+)

Sometimes there is a change in my schedule.(+)

I can stay happy if there is a change in my schedule.(-)

I can tell my teacher if I need help to be happy.(-)

I can still work at school even if there is a change in my schedule. (+)

Nice Mouth

I am nice with my mouth. (+)

My mouth is for eating.(+)

My mouth is for smiling.(+)

I am nice with my mouth.(+)

I will use my chewy or straw.(-)

I will be nice to myself with my mouth. (-)

I do nice things with my mouth. (+)

Friends at my House

I like it when my friends visit me at my house. (+)

We play with my toys. (+)

I keep my clothes on to play with my friends. (+)

If my clothes come off, I cannot play with my friends. (-)

I will be a good friend and keep my clothes on! (+)

My Helmet

I wear a helmet. (+)

Firefighters wear helmets.(+)

I will keep my helmet on.(-)

My helmet keeps me safe.(+)

Resources

For additional information and ideas I recommend the following online resources:

http://www.autismsociety-nc.org/ (information, services, conferences, online bookstore)

http://www.do2learn.com/ (games, resources, picture systems, learning tools)

http://www.iaba.com/ (Applied Behavioral Analysis)

http://www.mayer-johnson.com (Boardmaker)

http://www.pyramidproducts.com (PECS resources and training)

http://www.tasksgalore.com/ (curriculum & assessment materials for teachers and psychologists)

http://www.teacch.com/ (research, networking, and training about the TEACCH Program)

http://www.thegraycenter.org/Social_Stories.htm (Social Stories)

References

Agosta, E., Graetz, J. E., Mastropieri, M. A., & Scruggs, T. E. (2004). Teacher researcher partnerships to improve social behavior through social stories. Intervention in School and Clinic, 39, 276-287.

Barry, L. M., & Burlew, S. B. (2004). Using social stories to teach choice and play skills to children with autism. Focus on Autism & Other Developmental Disabilities, 19(1), 45-51.

Bledsoe, R., Myles, B. S., & Simpson, R. L. (2003). Use of a Social Story intervention to improve mealtime skills of an adolescent with Asperger syndrome. Autism, 7, 289-295.

Brownell, M. D. (2002). Musically adapted social stories to modify behaviors in students with autism: Four case studies. Journal of Music Therapy, 39(2), 117-144.

Crisis Prevention Institute (2004). Instructor manual for the Nonviolent Crisis Intervention® training program. Brookfield, WI: Compassion Publishing.

Del Valle, P., A. McEachern, & H. Chambers. (2001). Using social stories with autistic children. Journal of Poetry Therapy 14 (4): 187–97.

Gray, C. (2004). The Gray Center for social learning and understanding. http://www.thegraycenter.org/Social_Stories.htm

Gray, C. & Garand, J.D. (1993). Social stories: improving responses of students with autism with accurate social information. Focus on Autistic Behavior, 8(1), 1-10.

Gray, C. (1994). The new social story book illustrated edition. Arlington, TX: Future Horizons.

Gut, D., & S. Safran. (2002). Cooperative learning and social stories: Effective social skills strategies for reading teachers. Reading and Writing Quarterly 18: 87–91.

Hagiwara, T., & Myles, B. S. (1999). A multimedia social story intervention: Teaching skills to children with autism. Focus on Autism & Other Developmental Disabilities, 14(2), 82-95.

Hall, L. (1996). The generalization of social skills by preferred peers with autism. Journal of Intellectual & Developmental Disability, 21(4), 313-131.

Heflin, L. & Alberto, P. (2001). Establishing a behavioral context for learning for students with autism. Focus on Autism and Other Developmental Disabilities, 16(2), 93.

Horner, R., Carr, E., Strain, P., Todd, A., & Reed, H. (2002). Problem behavior interventions for young children with autism: A research synthesis. Journal of Autism and Developmental Disorders, 32(5), 423-446.

Ivey, M. L., Heflin, L. J., & Alberto, P. (2004). The use of social stories to promote independent behaviors in novel events for children with PDD-NOS. Focus on Autism & Other Developmental Disabilities, 19(3), 164-176.

Johns, B. (2004). Practical behavioral strategies for students with autism. Journal of Safe Management of Disruptive and Assaultive Behavior, 12(2), 6-11.

Kuoch, H., & Mirenda, P. (2003). Social Story interventions for young children with autism spectrum disorders. Focus on Autism and Other Developmental Disorders, 18, 219–227.

Kuttler, S., Myles, B. S., & Carlson, J. K. (1998). The use of social stories to reduce precursors to tantrum behavior in a student with autism. Focus on Autism & Other Developmental Disabilities, 13(3), 176-182.

Lorimer, P. A., Simpson, R. L., Myles, B. S., & Ganz, J. B. (2002). The use of social stories as a preventative behavioral intervention in a home setting with a child with autism. Journal of Positive Behavior Interventions, 4(1), 53-60.

Mancina, C., Tankersley, M., Kamps, D., Kravits, T. & Parrett, J. (2000). Reduction of inappropriate vocalizations for a child with autism using a self-management treatment program. Journal of Autism and Developmental Disorders, 30(6), 599-606.

Marshall, J. (2002). Parent-professional collaboration for positive behavioral support in the home. Focus on Autism and Other Developmental Disabilities, 17(4), 216.

Martin, G. & Pear, J. (2003). Behavior modification: What it is and how to do it. Upper Saddle River, New Jersey: Prentice Hall.

Mesibov, Gary (2004). Treatment and education of autistic and related communication handicapped children (TEACCH program). www.teacch.com, University of North Carolina at Chapel Hill.

Moes, D. & Frea, W. (2002). Contextualized behavioral support in early intervention for children with autism and their families. Journal of Autism and Developmental Disorders, 32(6), 519-533.

Norris, C., & Dattilo, J. (1999). Evaluating effects of a social story intervention on a young girl with autism. Focus on Autism and Other Developmental Disabilities, 14, 180-186.

Sansosti, F. J., Powell-Smith, K. A., & Kincaid, D. (2004). A research synthesis of social story interventions for children with autism spectrum disorders. Focus on Autism and Other Developmental Disorders, 19, 194-204.

Scattone, D., Wilczynski, S. M., Edwards, R. P., & Rabian, B. (2002). Decreasing disruptive behaviors of children with autism using social stories. Journal of Autism & Developmental Disorders, 32, 535-543.

Schopler, E., Mesibov, G.B., & Hearsey, K. (1995). Structured teaching in the TEACCH system. In E. Schopler & G.B. Mesibov (Eds.), Learning and cognition in autism (243-268). New York: Plenum.

Swaggart, B., Gagnon, E., Bock, S. J., & Earles, T. L. (1995). Using social stories to teach social and behavioral skills to children with autism. Focus on Autistic Behavior, 10(1), 1-16.

Thiemann, K. S., & Goldstein, H. (2001). Social stories, written text cues, and video feedback: Effects on social communication of children with autism. Journal of Applied Behavior Analysis, 34(4), 425-446.

Wallin, J.M. (2001). Social stories: An introduction to social stories. Online: www.polyxo.com/socialstories/introduction.html.

Whalen, C. & Schreibman, L. (2003). Joint attention training for children with autism using behavior modification procedures. Journal of Child Psychology and Psychiatry and Allied Disciplines, 44(3), 456-68.

www.ingramcontent.com/pod-product-compliance
Lightning Source LLC
Chambersburg PA
CBHW022133280326
41933CB00007B/667